CRAZY STAR

Rustin Larson

Loess Hills Books
Farragut & Shenandoah, Iowa

ISBN   0-9759439-1-X (paper)

Photograph of Rustin Larson by Terrence Kennedy

Cover art, woodcut, "Diver #5" copyright ©1998 by Jeanin Coupe
Ryding, used courtesy of the artist and Olson-Larsen Galleries,
West Des Moines, Iowa

Cover Design by Greg Tiburzi and
Clarinda Printing & Graphics, Clarinda, Iowa

Printing by Sheridan Books, Ann Arbor, Michigan

Publisher's Address   Loess Hills Books
                       PO Box 18
                       Farragut, Iowa 51639
                       (712) 246-3453 (fax & ph)
                       loesshillsbks@heartland.net
                       www.loesshillsbooks.com (website)

CRAZY STAR

Rustin Larson

ᥫᥫᥫᥫᥫ☀ᥫᥫᥫᥫ

Also By Rustin Larson

Loving the Good Driver
Islands (chapbook)
Lord of the Apes (chapbook)
Shimek (chapbook)
Tiresias Strung Out on a Half Can of Pepsi (chapbook)
Halves (chapbook)

for Caroline

Contents

Part One: Lord of the Apes

Part Two: Creatures Nobody Recognizes

Part Three: Beautiful Savior

Acknowledgments

Biography

Part One

Lord of the Apes

The Paternal Side

1840: bespectacled,
balding, hands quivering from too much coffee
as you sell peppermints in Larvik, Norway
to Kirsten, the grammar-school girl on her way

to the wharf with her grandfather's lunch
of kippers and goat's milk. You keep shop,
mildly educated, mind shadowed
by your God

and the thick black
hymnals on Sunday and the too-little-sugar
in your mother-in-law's apple pastry after
roasted snow goose and bitter ale. Your name

is Tomas, Edvard, Karl and Henry. You want
to travel to America and have a little more
land to raise your apprehensions, some new water,
diseases, smells to record

in your leaden book lying open
like the breast of a grave in snow,
a deep rectangle of relief before spring
in the short days of imperially-taxed

whale oil and tooth decay. You want to come
to Iowa to open a little grocery,
to be someone with a little power over destiny
and cheese as the sun illuminates

the lumber wagons, the stone crosses, the immaculate
   cash drawer.

Smoke, Black Shoes and a Red Airplane

Although I don't smoke, in dreams I do. Inhaling
the memory cloud, exhaling so clearly

the past liquefies as a bead of water on my glass
in the dining car of a train rolling through

the Tennessee morning. I smoke; my muscles relax;
my stomach unknots; I feel almost barefoot. The Negro

waiter clears my table and asks if I want more coffee.
I feel so good I offer him a cigarette he doesn't take,

so I sidestep down the narrow hallway to the smoking
car where everyone is so happy smoking and remembering

the last time they were honest, their smile in the shine
of their black shoes. We all smell of hair tonic;

a bald man smoking a pipe reminds me of my dad
under the Christmas tree, holding out one arm for me,

the other arm holding a sled while his teeth clamp an amber
cigarette holder. In the afternoon,

we go outside into the leaf-dead air to shoot turkeys,
and he teaches me how to smoke. The perfect white tube,

thin as a 12-year-old's ring finger. I cough and gasp,
but after a while I like it. I look up

and it's Wiley Post flying over our house in a red airplane—
the little airplane father landed under the Christmas tree

in 1934. Shivering in mid-air, propeller churning
the happy clouds of smoke, it shakes the snow down.

A flake melts in my hand into a glittering round coin. And I remember.

Harry James

It takes hard routes sometimes, this believing
your own life, like when you take your father
with you, 120 miles, to the site of your first
non-carcinogenic job, and he grumbles at the Hardee's
because they don't serve rolls at five in the afternoon,

you realize just how much of yourself has been struck
into the shining surface of that heavy old anvil.
You can bet he's fallen asleep on the way back,
mother driving to the silent radio, rain continuously
unzipping and zipping beneath the tires past the deer cross-
        ing

on Highway 34. Father is somewhere between
the way you hold your gut and the nicks you put in your
        face
while shaving. And you think of your own daughter
holding the door shut in front of you, saying, "Only people
can go through here! Not daddies!"

Sometimes at night you wonder, "Is that me breathing
when it rains like this, thinking any life is possible?"
$10 for that drop of water on the holly leaf;
$10 for that canister of skunk repellent;
$10 for that song on the radio. Harry James.

You can remember your trumpet teacher saying
you were going to be another Harry James.
And there was father going on about that ship of his
in the navy, 1943, about how he scrubbed the deck
of the McLanahan while James blared from the loud-
        speakers.

If life doesn't connect in circles, at least it spirals
upward and begins to sound really familiar; even the usual
complaints are like old friends. So at 5:00 p.m.
they don't serve rolls, and you're laughing
because you're so embarrassed, so proud.

High School

Once, in a class called Intro to Writing,
we watched a wordless film on the poetic image
in which botched developing
and pure, drug-influenced warp jumped freely
in and out of each other.
There was, at one point,
a go-go dancer—her face vibrating
like the business end of an electric sander.
The film freeze-framed: her wild hair
suspended motionless in blue space
as a superimposed hand soared in,
popped the top half of her skull
like a garbage can lid, and dropped in her
empty brain cavity two scoops of vanilla.
The lid of her head clicked down,
and she was back in business. "What

does this mean?" our genius of a teacher
asked. "What does this mean, Rustin Larson?"
Although, on the surface, I wanted to say, "It is
symbolic of the vacuous and purposeless energy
of contemporary youth which, in the eyes of the mature
          generation,
should supply a utilitarian purpose," I, instead,
uttered from the deepest corner of my self-consciousness,
"I dunno." "You don't know? Of all
the people in this class, I thought you
would know!" he said, totally shaken
and fizzed, as if the embarrassment
of his entire life accumulated into a Neapolitan
meltdown in his underwear that spotted
his gray hushpuppies;
as if I were supposed
to have a mop and bucket
in my pencil pouch.

The Lawn

Behind my house: a forest of sticks,
leafless, crowned with gray birds.
In front of my house, a beautiful
treeless lawn inclines roundly to an abrupt
horizon, which is why there is this feeling
of endlessness. Here you really get a notion
of the shape of the world, and understand
why no one else is around. Some may think,
"Oh, behind that hill are railroad tracks
connecting two great cities," or "Behind that
hill is a graveyard." What they don't know
about this lawn is it's the end
of all great destinations. Sometimes at night,
I feel as if I'm looking at another planet,
the grayness of dusk inhabiting the slow,
cold rotation. But in the morning I'm by myself:
playing Mozart on the phonograph,
brewing tea, going to pick white violets
that rest on the thick green like disabled stars.

The Recluse

what if we could take everything
that has ever been done to us
into the furnace of ourselves
and burn with it—
—*Glenn Watt*

Wound bleeding
her syllables
filled by such

a storm
of solitude.
Angel, look down

through the branches
at dusk.
Still

he can speak
as he burns
his letter to God,

to the insect
chirping love
with its glass-

green wings.

Trying to Save Brothers

1 *Washington, D.C. 1986*

So I'm on my way home on a hot May afternoon,
   the proverbial 102° in the shade;
     my car's air conditioner isn't working
    so it seems all my thoughts are coming back
from their orbit around the city and baking

into my flushed head: the morbidity of teaching
   freshman English, the unlikeliness of keeping my job
     at the community college north of town, thoughts of me
    noticing the traffic slowing down, thickening, thoughts of
         me
starting to feel trapped and edgy. It must have happened

just minutes before now, no cops around, no ambulance,
   just him with his face crushed to the pavement,
     blood raying out in all directions like a Japanese
    battle insignia, his motorcycle lying twisted near him,
the car, which he smacked broadside, straddling the curb,

a group of pedestrians gathering around, one even feeling
   the corpse's wrist and returning to the sidewalk,
     head shaking no, no. The dead man's long, blond hair
    shifts when a breeze puffs by; the fingertips
of his stiff hands press the pavement as if he were

about to push himself up and out of the accident,
   wipe his face on someone's shirt
    and be alive again.
   The driver in front of me grabs her mouth
when she sees it. And I, with all my shit-heeled thoughts

leveled to dust, steer forward, not thinking for a while,
  feeling the cry well in my chest,
    not because I knew him, but because
  whoever was angry last night when he came in late,
drunk and full of insults, whoever is washing

his stained sheets this very moment, doesn't have
  the slightest idea.

2 *Iowa, 1982*

I saw him that day, lounging
  in the library as I shelved books. What did he say
    to me? Something in Japanese and English.
  I shelving haiku, Konrad saying something to me
I'll never translate, something untranslatable

like drunkenness, like Pat firing into the dorm
  late that night, "Who's going to die next? You?
    You? Will it be you?" and I lying in my bed
  listening, staring at the blackened lamp, Pat breaking
a bottle on the doorstep and sitting down and crying.

I remember Konrad's girlfriend of a week (I once told him,
  "She's so cute, all she needs now are antlers,"
    whatever the hell that was supposed to mean)
  and Konrad dying before she could figure out if she
loved him or not, wandering the old campus of my memory

now, past the lantern erected in brick and iron
  for a drowning victim in 1925, a young man
    with a Greek name, Paupaulakos or something,
  drowned while he was trying to save brothers.
"No greater love does man know than this," says the bronze
      plaque.

Near the spot the huge oaks stop rustling, and someone
  is practicing cello in the conservatory, a third part
    for Brahms' German Requiem—
  all harmony, but recognizable as rain clouds
stir overhead making me choose between the student union

where *It's a Wonderful Life* is playing out of season
  for the sixth time this weekend, or the art studios
    where Pat is painting now—several weeks after
        Konrad's funeral—
  a portrait of a woman's torso, no face, but a cascade
of black hair over smooth boulders to a shining reservoir.

"I call her the mother of everyone," he says and invites me
  to sit down and sip beer he smuggled into the building
    in his "art" bag. It begins raining in earnest
  and the air becomes darker. I see our fluorescent
reflections in the streaming windows. It is late May.

In a few days we will be packing to go home,
  but we don't talk much now. I watch him paint,
    navel, contour of legs. This is life,
  this is what I need tonight,
her turbulent hair.

3 *Washington, D.C., 1986*

I am waiting for Caroline to come home, waiting alone
  in our room, in the air-conditioned gush of silence
    accompanying my thoughts. Was he nameless
  or am I feeling the loss of a brother, wanting him
back and living, even though he would grow to hate me,

call me a dipshit on a chance meeting in the supermarket
  as I fondle my way through a pile of cantaloupes.
    I want him back, even if this is a mercenary thought
  saying if he can escape it, so can I, so can Caroline,
the way we escaped the city once, driving to a place in
        Maryland,

a hamlet with stone houses from the Revolution...
  we pulled onto the shoulder, watched the sun go down,
    a broad field with a pond, some horses grazing
  far off...we were a little jealous we didn't own anything
so marvelous as these creatures silhouetted in day-end red,

wanted nothing but air between us and them,
  thinking, "This is what it means..." and "maybe this
    moment is the reason..." Pulling her close to me.
  Watching the sun and horses darken through a spray
of her hair.

Lord of the Apes

My aunt lived near a chemical plant
in a planned community
near a huge field
that grew nothing.

Every day her neighbor
would stand on his front stoop,
shirtless, beer in hand,
and yodel
that wounded animal-scream
of Tarzan.

I believe he did this
as an alternative
to blowing his brains out.

During his shift,
he helped produce
some miracle polymer
which would be transformed into the cockpit windows
of space shuttles.
My aunt had a slab of this stuff
smuggled from the plant.
She used it as a cutting board.
I think of this tonight as I slice broccoli
into little bits and scream
at my girls,
"Eat your veggies or I'll break your necks!"
and realize, for a split second
at the very least,
I really mean it.

My aunt was a barmaid
by profession. She served beers

to a species known for their
opposable thumbs.
And if I could perch on the porch
in my yellow skivvies
and roar like the Lord of the Apes
tonight in the frosty air
and make snow from my bad breath
and suffocate this whole neighborhood
of debtors and drunks
and violent cowards...well...

...who needs some damned
flowery metaphor
to give meaning to his life?

Sunday night, I had the kids tucked in
and there was this hysterical rapping
at the door.
I didn't want to answer it.
It terrified me.
But I turned on the porch light
and saw the iced-railing and steps
and standing there was a teenage girl
in a nightshirt
and pink naked legs
and no shoes and she was crying
and frightened so I opened the door
and I could smell Jack Daniel's
and she sniffled
and sputtered her boyfriend had been angry
and he punched his arm through a window
and now he was bleeding to death in their mobile home
and so I showed her the phone
and her fingers trembled as she dialed 911
and her knees wobbled
and she sat on the arm of the love seat
and held her forehead
and cried and cried

and said NO! when the dispatcher asked her
if she had tried to kill him
and she cried yes she cried flooding
my living room with vivid red
recollection as I heard the sirens coming
and I said I hear someone
and she clicked the phone down
and squeezed my shoulder when she passed
and said thank you
and I said good luck
and she closed the door
and separated the night outside
from the night within. So suddenly.

Snake Girl

She was the zookeeper's daughter
and sometimes her father
would bring a bag of snakes

to our school
and charm them
with an oboe.

I loved the way
the cobra spread its hood.
This was a dangerous school.

Not many children
were allowed to play
with Betty.

She would dress
their chimps
like little boys

and make us laugh
in the gymnasium.
Her father looked

like Darwin.
One year a chimp bit
off two of his fingers

and we all felt bad.
Another year, the cobra
bit him and we all said,

well, what do you expect?
Betty was thin and in 5th grade
had a flat chest.

The zookeeper in Omaha
had anti-venom and so her dad
lived his way out

of the coma. The next year
he brought cockatoos
to the gymnasium

and we were all fascinated.
He told us about
finches in the Galapagos islands

as he held up his hand,
two fingers invisible.
Feeling poetic one day

I told Betty
she had a divine light
in her eyes.

She turned toward
the drinking fountain
and held her hand over her mouth.

In a month her father took a job
at a large zoo in California.
And they were gone.

Lyndon "Beans" Johnson

Poor President Johnson chomped his nitroglycerin
and the journalists gasped. Hounddog head,
they replayed it at six and ten. I don't know
what season it was. If it were summer, we slapped
our feet on the cool mud under the swing set
and shot bottle rockets at the Red Baron.
Maybe the Baron would rage at the fence,
shaking his yodeling carpenter's saw. I suppose
there were many bombs and tanks and armored
personnel vehicles and helicopters twackthwacking
close to the earth. Through the blinds
we watched Tug's sister take off her bra
and gingerly dab on some cold cream.
The boy was being shipped out tomorrow
and everyone looked the other way except me.
It was necessary on those evenings to stay out long
after the stars appeared and shoot flakes
of burning trash at them. We burned old newspapers
to earn our quarters and we drank cold
Mountain Dew to keep our beds spinning
like propellers until the Bible verse was read
and Tug's sister said she could feel the baby
crawl inside her and Mr. Beans Johnson
would drawl to each of us, "My fellow
Americans..." and we could really taste it.

Cleo

was a basset hound, overweight, lazy
and sad.
She had gastric distress often, produced
horrible smelling farts,
vomited in great gushes,
left her crap in Dairy Queen swirls near my swing set
and everywhere else.
She chewed pork-chop bones
which she defended with low
barely audible growls, and
she would choke invariably
and stagger around the yard
making great rasping honks that nauseated me.
One day
a milk truck hit her
and broke her hip, and when she healed
she walked with her butt swinging sexily
like Susan Hayward in *I Want to Live!*
We kicked her away from our garbage
but she always returned, and since
she was not our dog
we could not kill her.

I want it to be clear
I harbored no love for this creature,
and when she died
I shed practically no tears at all.
It is only now
that I am middle-aged and ailing
I think of her with respect,
as I respect all of God's creatures,
including the unfortunate and broken.
If there is forgiveness
in memory,

let there be that and
all our bones dulled
by the teeth that erode,
the rains that come and
the sweet milk of the earth.

The Out-of-the-Body View from Stalag 17

Moments there made me talk
about the wood grain in the table,
how much it reminded me of myself:
those winter days I'd sit

on an ashen stump watching the harvested
cornfield not move. Those days,
I swear I heard every furnace
and stove burning along the country's north

edge until the stars came out,
and Dad came out to get me,
and we'd ride home, our faces ambered
by the radio light as the moon

sold well, an aspirin
curing the big one. I thought of fire
getting rid of old things—newspapers
and comic books: Captain America set free.

After dinner, we'd sit
in silence, only the sound of the burning
surrounding us. If we looked into
each other's eyes, it was the way

someone looked into a well: fearing,
longing. The night would crackle
and I'd pull the blanket up closer
to my chin, not knowing

I was growing older, not knowing the elms
were going to die, not knowing I'd travel
into the swirling alien night
and become a passenger of snow.

Away from Women

Two seventy-year-old brothers, a five-
year-old grandchild, suspend delicate

pendulums over the varnished water.
Here, there, slowly rising bubbles surface

spreading rings, concentric, undulant.
Away from women, far from brittle cups,

peach-blossomed paper coating bedroom walls,
translucent leaves, civilized elms, and oak

furniture gummed with thick ancestral smoke,
the brothers fish, amber whiskey passing and emptied

between them. Behind them sit the town's sun-
red houses; below them float their placid

bobbers. Not one damned bite.
Holding nothing innocence can't dissolve,

the boy sinks his line into the inlet's thoughts
and hooks out the water's brown-finned angel.

Part Two

Creatures Nobody Recognizes

The Nighthawk

(Jefferson County Hospital)

1

    A bat? Lonely above.
    Body and heart and soul.

    Its screech like a pulley drawing me up
    into the black
    and one street halo.

    Stuka buzz
    for some of the invisible,
    and hunger
    continues like a vein
    of combustible gold in stone

    as it always has; nurse brings in my tray
    of tenderized enigma
    and lima beans—I struggle
    with the plastic silverware &

    babblethink without enough
    evening to invade
    all the abstractions—Doctor C pops in,

    tells me about fishing
    the planet
    of philosophical trout

    where there was a shore
    of shattered blue glass
    where he cast
    for something pitiful.

His dialect spun
wildly like a reel
and he began to feel
he was some Portuguese facsimile

about to wind in his line
and vanish
witch-like into Akasha,
the memory of events

in the cosmos feeling
the void and trumpeting
its planetary jazz.

(The television hails
the genius of Louis Armstrong.)
Lonely like a fish lonely—

cascading out to stars like Niagara
and the way survival shows its face.
Its rugged shore.

2

Just shot an orange
with 12 units of sodium chloride.
This is practice for my next magic serum,
which I'll inject into my abdomen.
I get to pick a new district
of anatomy every week;
magic serum tends to make hardened

indentations in the skin,
which are ugly,
my educator grins.

She delights to mention my life span
has been shortened by decades,

that I might as well get used to death as a bunkmate.
Just shot an orange up,
12 units of sodium pentothal.
The bastard will never lie to me again.
Its bald porous surface
is to represent my skin,
so I snap the air bubbles from the syringe
and grin and drip rabies
onto the bedspread.
"This is good for you," I say to the orange.

"You are going to learn
a whole new way of life.
And you might even lose something—
because, after all,
isn't that what makes the bells ding
and the cocks crow
and the little breathy flowers to wake
in tears?"
The orange, like any good patient, accepts this—
because he didn't know he was killing himself—

and maybe he feels a little guilt
or grief deep down
in his blinding juice
and in his wrinkled little seeds.
He didn't know, the poor bastard, he didn't know,
and now he'll tell us everything. I throw
the needle into the BIOHAZARD box;
who knows, maybe the orange was HIV positive,

maybe too much truth
leaked out of the needle's
tiny hole, maybe we're all laughing
and feeling nothing

because death deals us numbers
we can't fathom.

3

Evening, and the clouds moving stately as ships
to war. The sun's benediction: this cause
is just or unjust. And others: thin wisps of vapor
so high they can never be history or any dreadful

lesson. The song to battle will have to be silence.
And the fields whisper for the waters,

a plummeting and continuous prayer.
Maybe in grace, maybe toward evening, I follow, oh wings.
And in the rainpipes, a whistling gravity of things
begotten with the clarity

of glass unearthed and cleaned to repeat
itself, a drink held and sweating,

and a flavor of love colonizing our senses
after a furious summer's day. Oh transcendence,
where are you? Are you the prayer I hear just awakening
in the nighthawk? Are you

the light I know seizing my body now, in this hospital,
my arms stuck with needles and my carnations withering

in an orange juice tube my daughter painted
into stained glass?
It is difficult for man to live
in both worlds, though I know the lovely dead

have heard me and in their brightness have lifted me up
like a pebble and turned me in their refining wings
and said, "Little thing,
oh little, little one..."

Creatures Nobody Recognizes

In the evening, alone together,
we eat our pauper soup.
On the radio, the music
of bowling balls rumbling
down a dark set of stairs
accompanies the excited cicadas. They rattle
until their skins burst, becoming
creatures nobody recognizes.
As the music falls asleep
into its black space, I think
of those creatures arriving into emptiness
the way a woman sings her way under
cool sheets.

I could spill my voice and burst
above your hurt glance which says
there's not enough money,
above your lips closed in a pout around the spoon,
above your eyes stubbornly holding back
their reservoir of starlight.
If I could burst through this shell
and be a boy again, I'd listen
to the rattle of cicadas. I'd pick their crisp
larval shells from the bark
of an elm. I'd ask those dried, split bodies:
what does the heart become
when it opens, and how will we
know it again?

Melons

You bought one, perfectly ripe,
but within days
little holes appeared
and it began to shrink from inside
like a consumptive.
Time after time we'd buy the sweet-smelling globes
and they'd rot.
You said we had bad luck with melons.
I said we were cursed,

and so it was we wandered the earth dreaming
of the perfect incorruptible melon.
We would walk by a woman
and think of melons. We would walk by a man
with large knees and think of melons.
Even when we were spending money on clothes
we would think we were dealing out melon leaves,
thick and prickly, always leaving
a trace on our hands. Our shoes became
melon rinds, and our fingers, slivers of ripe,
yellow melon. So when was it we stopped
thinking of these things? I think it was
the day in the supermarket when
you said to me, "Rus, I can't live
like this anymore!" and walked off,
leaving me to contemplate the absence of melons
and their traces, their juices and their mold.
"Why should I live like this either?" I thought,
and sat down on a crate, and weighed
my big round head in my hands.

Tiresias Strung-out on a Half Can of Pepsi

Today I sing about nothing, because it's
in front of me: crowbar, two flat balloons, empty flower

box, and a dozen cinnamon candies—like I said, nothing.
I sing of what I am, only this moment you're not

here, therefore
you are where you're not

since I imagine you here, or what you're not
since you're part of me. As I imagine your small rayon

blouse and your radiating smile, you aren't
really me, though you are,

which is amazing. Let me explain. Thirty minutes ago,
passing the tough crowd outside U-Wash-It,

I thought of you, and one thug seeing
your glow layered over my face hooted, "Nice Bod!"

So powerful is your absence, my life is endangered!
Homebound, I picked the glittering wrappers

of Butterfingers and Baby Ruths, hoping to discover
some special effect pertaining to me for a change.

And it was your face on all of them, hidden
in the vowels, visible when held to the sun

like Sandino in the white space of a 500 cordoba note.
Oh, I should have known you were trouble when I laid

eyes on you. You are the only thing I see now.
I play a record and it's your glassy eye spinning.

I drink milk,
and it's your operatic voice shattering the crystal

goblet inside my throat. "Come on," you are singing,
"be a man!" But as I stare into the mirror, already

I see the features of my face changing.

To Nort, with Vegetables

"Who has a question for Mr. Memory?"
            —*Stephen Wright*

I'm carving a beet, discarding the rough
outerskin, letting deep, red, vegetable-blood
run down my arm and drip into the stainless
steel sink. I hold the beet, admiring
the faceted, rinsed-glittering, the rings
of maroon penetrating it like psychic impulses
from Mars, long messages
of geographic and chronological details:

marker 212, Interstate 80, 1977, seventeen,
having learned to drive, speeding to Iowa City
to see you, to spend the weekend, to be kept up
half the night by pizza, and Steve who wants
to assure me Thomas Pynchon isn't anybody,
but a collective, the greatest ever, radiating
an intellect so vast the words never read
the same on the page twice; so I listen
rapt and unnerved by the wildly-animated voice,

unnerved by the walls of books radiating
their own bizarre energy, calmed somewhat
by my own thoughts already drifting to City Park
on Sunday afternoon, the crackling light and dirty
rugby players, the shouts of children running
toward the Ferris wheel, midget train, scrambler,
and the soda stand, the quench of lemon-
lime ice. There I am feeling the sun reflected off my white
shirt, reveling in the curved perfection of my
shoulders swelling for the girl in the white dress,
her clean hair abreeze as her electric-bulb chair
rotates down from the top of the wheel near the calm
river and trees lining the banks like some insomniac's

brilliant answer to sleep, a waking bout of unconsciousness
in my body, still whacked-out, years later, by speed,
my own naive ego on a self-proclaimed quest for God
alive in the bodies of women I'd never touch. I'm listening
to passages quoted rapidly, drinking bottles of Coca-Cola,
my eyes dimming under the lamplight, Steve's manuscripts
stacked hauntingly in the hallway toward the bathroom,
my sketchbook tucked in my backpack, your paintings
loose, everywhere, your ceramic amulets, balls of dust,
the dirty smell of old wildflower, meditations on the elastic
of my underwear begging to sleep on a dusty mattress.

The next morning, there you are making stir-fry:
chopping onions, peppers, mushrooms, crushing cloves
of garlic with a broad knife, tossing everything
into the sizzling black pan, saying, "Vegetables are beautiful.
They are like jewels," holding up a slice
of carrot like a ruby, holding it toward the window,
savoring the glow, saying, "Come here,
cook your own meal, you're old enough!" to me, sitting,
taunted by the uncarved.
So I enter the pungent steam
of garlic vegetables, appreciating them: sputtering
jewels, the frantic butter,
the festival of lunch, the gray
Sunday and October holding our lives,
the transmission of beets,
kingly and bleeding, treasures, messengers
from the liquid provinces of memory and love.

Something I Can't Touch

If it would snow, I'd go outside, scoop two white
handfuls and place them on my eyes.
I'd be calm and awake. The cold would seep
into my neurons and the things I'd remember would be
lit with the pure internal light of snow.

In Des Moines, in an opera house long ago,
I listened to the pines of Rome sprout
from papery seed to green swaying height,
and the woman next to me smiled
nervously because I kept glancing at her hands, and all the
        while
it was snowing outside, lightly,
and in each flake a line
in iambic pentameter settled and froze
on a parking meter while a bus leapt by full of sopranos
with red packages on their laps. When I got home
that evening I boiled some water
just to make the snow seem more intense. I imagined
the whole city smothered with dry white sugar.
That is why that day was so
important, because it was snowing

everywhere. I remember how I would go sledding head-
        first
down Break-Neck Pass, and how the snow would get
        scooped
into my sleeves and freeze into a ring of ice around
my wrists. I remember my wrists burning
and I wouldn't go inside until the lower
halves of my arms were numb. Sliding down the hill, over
and over, I would think of Charlie Chaplin's
gold rush shack teeter-tottering
on a cliff, like
a part of my life

just in front of me as I
flew down the hill, some part I could never quite
catch in time. Today
snow is something I can't touch but want to.
Half-formed, I know that part
I was always sliding toward is still here
in front of my face.
That is why today is so important.

Putting Up

The owner of the French Kiss saloon looked
at our sun-burned faces hoping we'd come

into his dark air conditioning, buy
$5 drinks and tell him what it was

like shooting the rapids. The rapids. Kind
of a joke since they were only ripples

on the Des Moines River, barely looking
like they'd rock our canoe. I told him, "No,

we're on our honeymoon and exhausted."
"As it should be," his little grimace said.

He let us go to our borrowed car to think
about where the keys were and how tired

"exhausted" means in the hottest August
in thirty years. Perhaps we wanted to give

flesh to the cliché of marriage being
a journey, etc., so we paralleled

the idea with a real river voyage
fed with more Huck and Jim clichés of our

single selves put to death, laid out in a canoe
like a pair of Viking marauders, drifting

and burning in the sun, the river, perhaps
a birth canal. When we put up in Bonaparte

at the wrong landing we were no longer
seeds, but actually felt lighter than the seed

that made us. When we dragged the canoe
into town we felt the weight of the new

body we had to share, the new head nearly
unbearable to lift at first, the new arms,

uncontrollable: mere weights flinging
randomly into rapidly cooling air. How

were the rapids? Over before we knew it,
but surprisingly strong, nearly impossible

to paddle upstream. We hugged the shore,
clung to branches, dug and scraped

our way. Putting up midway
at Bentonsport: no trace of a river-

boat landing, and only the limestone

remains of a mill. Old white houses
on the slope: lace-covered widows

shivering in the sun. A store displayed jars
of faded candy unopened since 1898.

If we had eaten that candy, one mothball-sized
piece would have drowned us in the bodies

of ancestors who sat by the river
on the sun-white grass, who died sweetly

at ninety, who dreamed their way
into river-town ghosts. Their gentle,

rippling laugh puts us to sleep
in the night of the complex joke

of life, or what appears to be.

Swallows

1

Spring. From our picture window

we watched them build the nest: the parents, dark blue,
pinching puddle-mud and grass.

When the nest became dry,
the mother became a small head in a turret.

November, the first black ice took over
wheel ruts. Pickup trucks swooped down the gravel road,

loose strands of hay rattling
the dry beds.

I recalled how swallows fluttered under the overhang
until the young could fly,

then father knocked the nest down with a shovel.

2

We look out the window, see ourselves
staring back, seated at the table.

The soft, yellow light overhead
makes everything warm and safe.

On television, helicopters are landing;
camouflaged soldiers scramble through a field

of tall yellow grass. Sister reads from her textbook
and talks about negotiations in Paris.

Father, the American, says nothing.
Brother will go to college next year,

join a fraternity
of budding professionals.

3

Dear Brother,

Five new ones this spring: mouths open,
noiseless, always waiting. The mother

goes about her work
without a sound,

killing an English sparrow that flies under the nest.
The young birds are desperate for food.

Your first postcard came from Saigon, today.
I love the dark birds wheeling in its glossy blue.

When the season ends,
there will probably be only two fledglings

from the five speckled eggs.
I seem to find a new one every day: eyeless,

nub-wings hugging
the sidewalk.

Disrupted Peace

Forget the crickets buzzing
their socket wrenches
in the peonies-turned-tinder,
or the toads with their bubble-gum
throats and warty brown sacks
of paralysis and hallucinations,
but remember the few strobes
of heat lightning kinetiscoping
the backyard: the marmalade
cat eunuch caught mid-leap
out of the junipers,
something silvery and obscure
tentacling in its mouth:
flickety-flickety and stone motion.

Let this be the black summer
you've died for.
Let the mind smash a brick
through the window of heaven.
Let Christ crumple his newspaper
down into his lap, mash
his cigarette in his Sea-
World-of-Texas ashtray.
Let him thunder: "This comes out
of your allowance, young man!"
Let the cat blend into lightning.
Let the birds fly away.

Crazy Star

When I arrived at your door in Brooklyn Heights,
your cat stared at me through the bars
of your street-level window, through the junked
Honda and the trash cans always queued for pickup.
"I want bad news," his eyes seemed to say.
Above me one crazy white star
was beginning to wear a hole in the sky's cloth.

I had been fired from the Institute
of Biological, Mental and Social Misfits.
Their residence was situated in the midst
of a howling cornfield smack dab in the center
of nothingness. The occasional bus
would come and go, dropping off transfers
from the county jail or state mental hospital.
Believe it or not, there was a tall Indian
who said nothing just like in that movie.
But instead of smashing a window with a water fountain,
he would lie for hours unchained under the poplar tree
and move his legs like a dog having a really good dream.

My job was to teach them all something
real—magic tricks—turning pockets
full of change into cigarettes or tasty items
from the menu of forbidden food.
This I would sometimes do.

But mostly I would shuffle them
on a field trip schedule and hope
they didn't stink up my car
on a ride to the corner five-and-dime
in a town miles distant and askew.

There was Bread & Jam Mary who confided
she once shot a man in the leg.

She said this at the VFW over a tenderloin
and a Pepsi—her adventure in budgeting
for the month. "I had to do it,
Rush. He shaid he going to take me.
And I didn't want to be took. Show I drilled
thish here hole in hizh leg, shee?" She whistled
and wheezed, revealing a mouth of ruin.

I looked around the VFW, the tobacco stench
and Budweiser neon, and remembered
this was the literary pub tour of Southeast Iowa.
Phil Stong used to drown his sorrows here.
Town Legend: after *State Fair* was published,
none of his other books did well.
In his day a person could ask, "Where's Phil?"
and the usual response: a pantomime bottle
tipped to the mouth and chugged with a gluck,
gluck, gluck bobbing adam's apple.

"God, I wish I could have one hard drink," Mary said.
I bought her one.
"Gee, I could marry a guy like you, Rush."

In Brooklyn Heights under the crazy star
I thought about Phil Stong and failure and Mary
as your cat glowed at me.
I was thirsty. I didn't know where to buy a drink.

The Korean cabby who thought I was a queen
took my last $20 and drove off only to be shot
in the chest late that chilly Tuesday night
near La Guardia by a murderer who blended
perfectly with the jumble of construction
and steaming manholes.

A really nice Italian woman
screamed something at me
from across Clinton street.

You weren't home and I had no idea
where I was going to sleep, or what luminescence
would swallow me.

A Woman Praying to Her Umbrella

There is a woman praying
to her umbrella—her hands
clasped around the handle
and her forehead pressed
against her hands. Her eyes
are closed, I can almost see
them fluttering, though I know
she is deep in prayer
to her god who has something
to do with rain or staying dry.
There are many people on this train—
they all have their little umbrella-gods,
though not all of them are praying
as fervently as this brown woman
in front of me. Perhaps she is praying
for me, who forgot my umbrella,
or, omnisciently, for my wife
who also forgot her umbrella,
who is driving to the dentist
elsewhere in the city, on this
gray wet morning which appears
to want to bless us equally.

Part Three

Beautiful Savior

Ice at Midnight

Say you stayed
and the world had turned
out all right,

say you had the choice
between the green blouse
and the white sweater,

say you poured Total
into a cold china dish
and gave thanks to the milk,

say the light was right
and you could see the men
clearly on the golf course

on the far hill,
say the world was offering
a special on faces

and tomorrows,
say the first one in a million
got a free sponge bath,

say the radio played
all day each song you adored
in 1960,

say the Air Force jets were climbing,
cheerful and loaded,
say it was a day with one cloud

and the medicine
of the wind sang
in the clotheslines,

say the curve of light
was a knife with which you cut
through your own sighs

and served them high
to your ladies
with whipped-cream

and a dazzling new
green punch
from *Woman's Day,*

say you could have gone on and on
with just a gallon
left in your VW

and a coupon for a free wash and wax
at Kincaid Standard,
say the burgers were frying all day

at The Drummer Boy and you decided
cooking was for the birds,
say your menu was whatever

kindness called on the black telephone
during Dialing for Dollars,
say you loved us all,

especially me, say you said that
tree was heaven and that stone
and that voice on the radio

urging us all to stand by for a test
of the Emergency Broadcast System,
say it never happened

and you are sitting
here with me, watching me as I drink
ice at midnight

and as I write
to an empty plate of crumbs
and you tisk

and say how I was once
a handsome young man
and how sad it all is.

Mr. Mom

Basically all institutions, marriage,
religion, government, are designed
to give you an ulcer and eventually destroy
you from the inside out. This I
believe is one of the missing wisdoms
from Blake's Hell. The house tonight
seems like an ice-locked freighter.
The rain types gently on the roof.
I believe tonight we are the rain's
manuscript. I believe we forever
will be. The crickets' relentless
chirring is packed with subliminals.
As they said in *Charlotte's Web*, "Summer
is dying, dying..." And I remember
my sweet wife laughed at the emotive whisper
with which I read that to my daughter,
which daughter I now cannot remember.
Life is chock full of cheap crimes.
There's the oven, one demon snarls,
go stick your head in it. By weird twists,
I had become a male housewife, reviled,
ridiculed. One testicle shrank
to almost nothing, the other had a huge
ego. Changing the diapers of my baby girl,
I sang along with David Bowie, "I'll be
a rock'n'rollin' bitch for you."
And she smiled a bubbly-blue, toothless coo.
I never answered the door in an apron.
But I made one casserole of a hell.

Pleasant Plain

Let's round it off and call it 2 a.m. The rumble of a truck down Pleasant Plain Road. I look out and our streetlights say nothing but their usual advertisement for mute space. I hear the horn of a distant train, its romanticism or remoteness, its people struggling in berths, and perhaps one insomniac like me nursing a tiny bottle of Grand Marnier in a club car (if they exist anymore) or at a table of the train's snack car, looking out the window at all the obscurity and lights. This would be a Midwestern train, barreling through all but a few towns to Chicago—none of the slowing and uncoupling and waits by vacant (but for a man or woman) plat-form, such as north of NYC—posters of the latest musical, *Cats* still on kiosks throughout the station. Yes, the diesel rumble was Amtrak, but heading west this time to Omaha. The earth is turning. It's the vacant winter months before spring training (no pun) and the lazy crackle of AM radio broadcasting the St. Louis Cardinals. I don't know any of the players' names. I don't care. And yet base-ball is something to massage the mind, like solitaire, when you can't find one thread, one decent image. The old dude across the street sawed his apple tree down. Just a ground level stump. I don't know what this means. I see him, half-blind, walking his terrier in the yard, daily. I see his brother with the huge tumor on his back pick up twigs. I smell their wood stove burning. These aren't things, but homogenous realities. One couldn't exist without the other. Our pet rat, Nick, scratches behind his ear. He takes a few hits from his water bottle. My hand grows numb. Usually a train is an image for some unsolvable spiritual journey, but tonight I am just a tunnel and all that luggage going to Omaha barely notices me, although I must have sounded like a tune one passes through by accident and then finds everyone else is singing at the newsstand, or the coffee shop in harmony with the anguished "OOOOOOOO!" of donuts frying.

Islands

The neighbor's springer spaniel looks
bored. She's made a nest of mown
grass and she lies in it. The sky
is interspersed with an armada of
silverfish. The blue
between is pale and fragile.
The heat is endless. The spaniel walks
in and out of her sky-blue dog
house. On a terraced garden nearby
are marigolds and thousands of
cherry tomatoes sweet and perfect as
red pearls. The springer spaniel keeps
circling. There is a drunk in a lawn
chair watching her. He is bare-
chested with a huge beer gut. He
is wearing rainbow swim trunks. He
is the owner of the hot and bored
spaniel. It is 92 degrees and the
humidity is like a rubber suit.
The leaves of the olive tree twitter
with a slight breeze. A yellow butter-
fly chases nothing across the barren
yard. Now the branches of the tree
seem to be nodding yes. And even some
distant fir trees seem to stir like
a scrotum kissed by the neighbor's
wife. Distant, an abandoned farm's
windmill spins and spins only to say
the wind is from the south. Now
the clouds' shapes have changed. They
seem like islands in the tropics.
More, they seem like the ghosts
of islands, if islands could die and choose
the ocean above as paradise to be and ease
to our lives here deep below.

Turboprop

Before the world got so freaking ambitious,
an evening's entertainment in our city of morons
would be buying a bag of burgers and fries
and parking out by the runway
to watch the planes take off and land
on their field strung with starry blue and
white and red lights. Some summer's
dusk—and no one had to admit their hearts
were filled with departure. Cheerleaders
would park their asses on the hoods
of Impalas and dream of getting it
in pressurized cabins 10,000 feet and climbing.
Housewives would scheme one well-planned
rendezvous in Mexico whose sunset would be
calmer than Seconal and a salve to each
abscessed scar. And every husband would gleam
at the ivory nose of the Ozark turboprop
and think of the right bra cup
of a stewardess demonstrating the proper
method of disrobing in the event
of a water landing. Oh, the hours spent
in a life raft—clothed in nothing but Coppertone.
But we children, dressed early in our baseball
jammies, would gum our salty fries and sip
our shakes and plug our ears to the windy roar
of the Ozark whose windows were lit
to the tired August dusk. You could catch
glimpses of faces of men and women strapped
in and grimly prepared for takeoff,
the substance of their lives being drawn
backwards by the force of gravity,
their bodies leaving the ground,
uncertain and liberated.

Libraries, Librarians, Shelves, Clocks, Balconies

George Bailey, in the altered universe
where he doesn't exist,
threatens to pummel Clarence
the guardian angel
unless he reveals the whereabouts
of Mary, George's not-wife.
"You're not going to like it, George!
She's just about to close the library!"

And there she is, eye bags heavy
with a day of shushing patrons,
her skin the olive hue of leather-bound classics,
and she screams because she doesn't like
the looks of a man wild-eyed and sweaty
from the hard labor of having no identity,
let alone a library card.

"Mary, Mary! I love you! I need you!
Our children! Mary!" George shouts
and Mary swoons
giving birth to a cavern fluttering
with abstractions and dark facts.

And isn't this the way we all feel?
And when she treats us coldly with a smirk
and a smudged due date at the circulation desk,
doesn't our passion for her mysterious
existence grow even more fervent?

Parse the sentence of your life and see
if the subject does not lean toward her
the way an amaryllis aims
its expectant pod of blossoming toward the sun.

Today I walk into the library
and walk out hostage to an armful
of books. The police
roll slowly by as I let myself
into my car, the corner of Emily Dickinson
pressed to my temple:
stay calm and no one gets hurt.

I see the lights go off in the library
and then back on again.
Fifteen minutes till closing time.
George Bailey looks wild-eyed
as half his face revolves from shadow
like a reference section globe.
"Fifteen minutes till closing time, George."
Clarence tugs on George's sleeve.
"No! No! Dog gone it, no!" George says.
"Mary! Mary! My card! Where did I put my card?"

1984, The Library of Congress: My Lunch with Richard Wilbur

Nobody in the world knows or cares,
but in my spare moments I am working
on a piece in blank verse called "Father,"
though it isn't my father conjured there
but someone who reads Macbeth. It's my usual
turkey on rye with large soda with ice
twinkling like that section of ocean

that swallowed the Titanic. And far
as I know, the whole table is mine and the view
of the church spire, and the freeway,
and the general tachycardia of D.C.
High atop the library's Madison Building
in the cafeteria, and my heart flutters
a little because who is heading straight
for my table but Anthony Hecht,
Congress's Consultant in Poetry,
gray lion's head in a red bow tie,
navy-blue blazer and glimmering black shoes.

I'm just a clerk in Labor Relations—
he hasn't a clue about "Father"—
and he leans toward me and asks, "Would you care
terribly if I seat a few of my friends
at this table?" which in retrospect, I'm sure,
translates, "Would you please leave?"
But I wave my open palm over the tabletop
like a sultan to indicate it is no skin
off my weasel who sits to my front
or to my side. And so, rolling his eyes,
Hecht motions for his entourage to come
forward—a boy, my age, with rotten teeth
and crutches; a white-haired woman;
and the poet, the guy I want to be when I grow up,

his face unmistakable–they kerplunk their lunches
down at the table. I stare out
the window again, knowing for certain
I'm too scared to say anything.

Turning to my sandwich, though, I see his tray
and notice the slicked steak on French bread,
the fries, the coffee, the little slice
of pecan pie. He bites into the sandwich
as though half his mouth is in abscess,
and I think, "This is how a real poet eats."
The rotten boy turns

to the poet on eager rump and says,
"Tell us about the time you went sailing
with JFK." And the poet inhales
like a lost cavern of gold and sighs,
"Ah yes, Jack loved his boat."
I feel the crisp pages of "Father" poking blindly
from the inside pocket of my blue jacket.
I pull the artifact and unfold it.
I say, "Oh, sir!" and he looks at me kindly.

"I just want you to know I know who you are
and..." I stumble on, "I am a poet, I've begun
to be, sir. I was wondering if you would sew
your opinion on this, Mr. Merwin?" Mid-chew,
his eyes widen to moons and he coughs like a gun.
Never since have I seen steak fly so far.

A Fog Wanders

The rabbit angrily yanks the parsley
from my hands with his teeth.

The night slowly freezes.

Above the streets
a fog wanders.

If I shouted from this porch
only the shout would answer.

And what noise
deserves to be so lonely?

The Town Where John Logan Was Born

Desolation
              and leaves, syntax
                          of drift.

Joy Street.
              Loudest thing
                          in this town: the dark

blue west.
              Tavern's neon-green
                          mouth smiles, drinks.

The trembling
              of a chin,
                          this avocation

bitter, illicit.
              "Heart to Heart
                          Talk to My Liver,"

Dead man's lips.
              Red Oak. Orange
                          water tower full

of cyanide.
              Your books?
                          Don't bother

to look
              in the stores
                          on the crumbling

square.
              You are not,
                          nor ever will be,

a hero here,
      a town proud
            of cultural

suicide.
      Hitchhiking
            for something

divine,
      an intervention,
            Joy Street,

the blue west,
      the loveliest thing
            sometimes

the deadliest.

Beautiful Savior

I want black Jesus above the doorway
with the palm leaves and the rusty nails
I pulled from the two-by-four that lay
derelict in the burdock.
I want his skin licorice and his beard a shock
of snow. I want his eye whites
black marbles and his irises white
as amphetamines.
I want his robes to be the night:
starless, moonless.
I want his sandals
to be my walking long past
the clock tower and the small hand
accusing the numerals that stutter I...I, I...I, I, I...

Spillville

to Antonin Dvorák

1

In this small Iowa town,
grandmothers and housewives
in leaf-and-bird-embroidered dresses
serve paprikash and kolache,

setting the hot bowls and cool trays
on folding tables on the school playground.
The guests of honor: "The Composer's
String Quartet," all the way from New York City

to commemorate your birth
in concert at St. Wenceslaus Church
where, on the summer Sundays of 1893, you

played the organ. The church is pink
sandstone settling into a hill
covered by cedars. I walk through the graveyard
where the bones of Catholics

knead themselves into the dark
soil. And as I enter the church,
the soprano sings, "Death reigns
in many a human breast," though

in German. I read
the program's English translation.
Who wrote
these words?: "Wasted

and desolate the heart is.
Dead all its life
of joy unblest..." Did people

in the late 19th century depend upon these verses

as a habitation
for their loneliness?
I look about the church and realize the people
this sad music was intended for.

Near the musicians
glows the undisturbed
marble of Christ's image,
and of Mary's whose face heals the sick

and is always younger than her son's. The music
laps like waves on the sanctuary's
plaster walls, "...happy visions rise
again," the big woman sings,
dreaming happily of her enormous love.

2

Homesick, anxious to speak your language,
you spent one summer eighty-nine
years ago in this Bohemian settlement,
and they honor you with this festival.

This small church echoes
with your Piano Quintet in A Major,
the black-gold trilling

of a meadowlark faintly rises through
a sanctuary window and mixes
with violin and piano. The world is green now,
sun-fed. Music aches

and wanders the dense foliage
of Turkey River valley, where you
wandered, where gray birds sprinkle
through a half-light of oak leaves.

This place was enough
to keep you. The people
you spoke to were peasants,
farmers. Perhaps

you enjoyed best talking
to them about the virtues
of coarse bread, or what to swallow
for a cough, or who could remember

what the morning air smelled like
outside of Prague, a hundred
kilometers from the city
where pockets of purple loosestrife blossomed.

3

This is the brick building
where you lived one summer
on the second floor, the first floor
now a museum for clocks ornately carved

by the Bily brothers.
On the stroke
of an hour
a miniature

Washington tosses a cherry pit from Mount Vernon,
little Abe steps from his White House door
with a draft of the Emancipation Proclamation
(the parchment like a fingernail in his delicate hands.)

There is even a violin clock carved to honor
you. You wouldn't have slept with all
these pendulum clacks and hourly clangings,
cuckoos, rattles of springs. All this time

announces to itself that it is indeed time,
but for what? You
were in your humid apartment with one simple clock,
sketching the new world, striking time

signature, dotting notes
on coarse tan paper. Your steel nib
rasped American Negro spirituals, hymns
of prairie churches. You looked up briefly

at gray locust shells clinging to black
tree limbs, as summer was one huge brush
of green. Twenty-eight years
after Lincoln's death,

you filled your music with tobacco ooze
of American voices and Bohemian voices
whose crystal wings still shatter
on the ceiling of a dawn-pink church.

The Yorba Linda Blues

No angel scrolled gurgling columns of music
in his ear for this one.
And he cooled himself on no stone balcony
of spouting gargoyles
but by the window of his unremarkable house,
with his dishwasher, who he named Patricia
Nixon, churning in the background, Protestant
and rhythmical as the screws of a destroyer
furrowing the Pacific for Shinto periscopes.

He wanted to be at balance with the wind spirit's universe,
so he shouted out the window, alternately,
"Forgive me!" and "Damn you!"
into the cool black May air
and heard his echo batted back by the pine windbreak
a quarter mile off, under which he knew
his children were inhaling the levitating red
coals of their bewilderment.

Lord, he knew the foliage
must have been bleeding from its pain-filled,
ear-like eyes, noses and throats.

Oh, holy children,
forgive your father, heavy with an ass's war
and ready to die for all the wrong reasons,
his voice like a hammer thrown to kiss the nursery windows,
and his hands...his horrible stone hands...

*Yorba Linda is the birthplace of President Richard Nixon.

Imitations

A bit like the cellophane used in plays
to imitate the surface of water,
the skin of the river glimmers—
a bit like birds that hover, lost in the power
of flight, the wavelets flash—
or like a glade ignited with lightning—
or like a handsome man
rotting in maximum security, with the glazed
tiles of the walls reflecting the single bulb
and reminding him of the diamond-like river
he used to swim in as a boy, how his
wet body flamed on the shore, a child
of living light—something like the hole
in the cloud from which Jacob's ladder beams
and imitates the spray of a garden
hose set on fierce, out of which arc jewels
the daughter he murdered once caught
in her open hand.

He Can Barely Speak

He can barely stand.
　　　My father, having refused
　　　　　the nursing home,

is ending his days
　　　in a crust of dried fecal matter
　　　　　on his couch.

The television has been switched
　　　by my daughter
　　　　　from a golf tournament

to a play: *look love what envious*
　　　streaks do lace the severing
　　　　　clouds in yonder east.

"Who writes this crap?"
　　　"Shakespeare, Grandpa! Shakespeare does."
　　　As Frank O'Hara

once wrote: *prince of calm*
　　　treasure of fascinating cuts
　　　　　on my arm.

You have been my father.

Something About Life

At the vegetable stand in Richmond,
they did good business
because what they sold

was outdoors.
It was plums,
apples, peaches, tomatoes,

the proximity of sunlight.
In their pine wood crate
were the onions: the sweet kind

people eat for breakfast.
We bought a honeydew that rotted
in the heat of the window

on the drive back to Washington.
But the things we saved were sweet...
nectarines which the bees

wouldn't leave alone.
We had handpicked, looking for scars,
a watermelon which I thumped

for density and ripeness.
It thumped dull and resonant
like a muffled drum. I ate it

when I was sick, feeling cured
from the red core.

Tell Me About the Wasp Again

for Jacob Godwin-Jones

The brown wasp clinging to the porch screen?
He was awakened, fooled by warm weather.
Today, February blossoms: the wasp
looks at you and me who smash flowers
on the porch steps with a round stone.
Perhaps he wonders what we will do with all
the green nectar, or worries we will exhaust
the yard of white flowers he has some claim to.
So, maybe we are not being fair; maybe
we cannot reassure him that before long we
will tire of it.
                    He is staring at you,
Jacob. You could squash him with a blow
of your tennis shoe. You could blow on
the screen and he would fly away.
Maybe he would jab one of us with his stinger—
the fine brown barb with a sack of poison that throbs heart-
        like
when its shaft is stabbed in flesh—but who says
we can't inhabit the same triangle of time unharmed?

We will not tap the screen
where the wasp suns himself. We will watch
as he builds his house from mud; the same mud
we were, Jacob, before these bodies
were spun, and our souls poured into them.

Something Visceral

In this amber cubical on earth,
on a Thursday evening as it rains,
in a library near the books that deal

with the Mafia and finance,
as the trade centers lie in smoke and ruin,
I, in Iowa, with a few voices,

and answers speaking to nothing
immediately near: the seeds the squirrels hoard,
the grasses still green, the apples

luxuriant again following a foul year.
Can we believe it all to end too soon?
We who feel, who can't let go of the body,

so it becomes the only song we sing,
though the rapture extends its great fiery arms,
though it extends its engulfing sleeves,

and the Lord smiles, and everything these
Jehovah's Witnesses painted on their pamphlets
comes true, still

we the singers, the true sinners and lovers
of earth, remain coaxing a tyrant death
to sleep with our silent sibilance,

our thoughts, our rhythms and shaking;
though our teeth become castanets
and our intestines the strings

of hideous guitars,
we sing, we sing, and we
will not let go.

Acknowledgments

Gratitude is expressed to the following publications where some of these poems first appeared:

The Amherst Review "Snake Girl"
Arsenic Lobster "Beautiful Savior"
Atlanta Review "Librarians, Libraries, Shelves, Clocks Balconies"
Beyond 9-11 "Something Visceral"
Calliope "1984, the Library of Congress: My Lunch with Richard Wilbur," "Trying to Save Brothers," "Swallows"
Cimarron Review "Harry James," "High School," "Imitations," "Melons," "The Yorba Linda Blues"
Defined Providence "Disrupted Peace," "The Recluse," "To Nort, with Vegetables"
Diner "Lyndon 'Beans' Johnson"
Embers "The Out-of-the-Body View from Stalag 17," "Smoke, Black Shoes and a Red Airplane"
The George Washington Review "Spillville"
The Iowa Review "The Nighthawk"
Loonfeather "A Woman Praying to Her Umbrella," "Creatures Nobody Recognizes," "Something About Life," "Tell Me About the Wasp Again"
The MacGuffin "Islands"
Mankato Poetry Review "Putting Up"
Midwest Quarterly "Turboprop"
Natural Bridge "The Town Where John Logan Was Born"
The North American Review "Cleo"
The New Yorker "The Paternal Side"
Panoply "Away from Women"
Passages North "Floaters"
Poetry East "The Lawn"
The Poetry Miscellany "Tiresias Strung-out on a Half Can of Pepsi"
Rhino "Mr. Mom"
The Washington Review "Something I Can't Touch"

The Worcester Review "He Can Barely Speak"

Some of the poems in this book also appeared in:

The Dryland Fish (1st World)
Eclipsed Moon Coins (Blue Light Press)
Loving the Good Driver (Mellen Poetry Press)
Voices on the Landscape: Contemporary Iowa Poets (Loess Hills Books)

The poem "Tiresias Strung-out on a Half Can of Pepsi" originally appeared in **The Poetry Miscellany** and also appeared in **Collecting Moon Coins**, an anthology published by Blue Light Press.

"The Paternal Side" originally appeared in **The New Yorker**. Copyright 1992 by *The New Yorker* Magazine, Inc.

Thanks to Michael Carey for his suggestions and for the sequencing of the poems in this book. Thanks also to Robert Long, Michael Carrino, Walter Butts, Bill Kemmett, Jack Myers and Charlie Langton for their support, comments and encouragment.

Biography

Rustin Larson's poetry has appeared in *The Atlanta Review, The Iowa Review, The North American Review, The New Yorker, Poetry East,* and other magazines. *Loving the Good Driver,* his first full-length book of poetry, was nominated for The America Awards in Literature and was a finalist for the New Issues Poetry Prize. Larson's other poetry collections include *Tiresias Strung Out on a Half Can of Pepsi* (Blue Light Press, 1993), *Islands* (Conestoga Zen, 2002), and *Lord of the Apes* (Conestoga Zen, 1999). Larson was a featured Iowa Poet at The Des Moines National Poetry Festival in 2002 and has been featured on the public radio programs *Live from Prairie Lights* and *Voices from the Prairie.* Currently, Larson teaches in the English department at Kirkwood Community College in Cedar Rapids, Iowa and lives in Fairfield, Iowa with his wife, Caroline, and their three daughters.

The Loess Hills Poetry Series

Voices on the Landscape: Contemporary Iowa Poets
edited by Michael Carey, 1996

Winter in Eden — Robert Schultz, 1997

Across the Known World — Keith Ratzlaff, 1997

Keep Silence, But Speak Out — Charlie Langton, 1998

In Divided Light — Jan Weissmiller, 1999

Crazy Star — Rustin Larson, 2004

Loess Hills Books

is located in Shenandoah & Farragut, Iowa and is dedicated to the best in contemporary American fine arts writing.

Its books are a gift from the people and businesses of the the Essex, Farragut, Red Oak, Shenandoah, Sidney & Villisca community and the City of Shenandoah including:

Jacky Adams
Robert & Evelyn Birkby
William & Jan Billings
Jean Braley
Gregg & Elaine Broermann
Loreen Burrichter
Drs. Donald & Janet Bumgarner
Michael & Kelly Carey
Dr. Skip & Mary Jo Carrell
Elizabeth Chick
Gregg Connell
Barbara Cunningham
William & Laura Danforth
Dr. Robert & Colleen Dostal
Alan & Belinda DeBolt
Joseph & Julia Denhart
John Dilg & Jan Weissmiller
Eaton Corporation
The First National Bank (of Farragut & Shenandoah)
Richard & Dixie Fishbaugh
Friends of the Shenandoah Library
Dr. Tim & Lisa Fursa
Jan Frank-de Ois
Dr. Kenneth & Jean Gee
Philip & Mary Anne Gibson
David & Faye Hankins
Linda Henderson
Kurt & Mims Henstorf
Jack & Becky Hoenshel

C.E. & Carol Hornbuckle
Howard & Mary Alice Johnson
Jay & Jary Johnson
Dr. Floyd & Sue Jones
Bruce & Sara Ketcham
John & Diane Kidd
Gary & Mem Laughlin
Earnest & Jeannine Liljedahl
Robert & Ellen West Longman
Tom Lynner
Dale & Clara Jane Matthews
Dale Matthews
Ed & Carolyn May
Jake & Pam McGargill
Lee & Virginia Gingery
Doris Mc Neilly
Jim & E. Vee Myrberg
Robert & Edi Norris
Mary Jean Offenburger
Robert & Sharon Paulus
Pella Rolscreen Foundation
Nancy & George Perry
Richard & Nancy Profit
Robert & Debby Rake
Cy & Carolyn Rapp Charitible Trust
Dennis & Linda Reilly
Reilly Insurance Agency
Robert & Maribelle Read
The City of Shenandoah
Shenandoah Family Dentistry, PC
David & Edy Shull
The Sidney Argus Herald
Sorenson Auto Plaza
Brad & Tammi Sorenson
Jeff & Vickie Suchomel
Barb Sjulin
Mark Heininger & Jennifer Seydel
John & Gayle Teget

Charles & Mary Williams
David & Corrine Williams
Loche Williams
Robert & Carol Wolford